JAN DARRYL

VEGETABLE GARDENING

The Essential Guide To Vegetable Gardening for Beginners, Discover How to Start Your Own Vegetable Garden and Save Money Growing Your Own Vegetables!

Descrierea CIP a Bibliotecii Naționale a României
JAN DARRYL
   VEGETABLE GARDENING. The Essential Guide To Vegetable Gardening for Beginners, Discover How to Start Your Own Vegetable Garden and Save Money Growing Your Own Vegetables! / Jan Darryl – Bucharest: Editura My Ebook, 2021
   ISBN

JAN DARRYL

VEGETABLE GARDENING

The Essential Guide To Vegetable Gardening for Beginners, Discover How to Start Your Own Vegetable Garden and Save Money Growing Your Own Vegetables!

My Ebook Publishing House
Bucharest, 2021

TABLE OF CONTENTS

Chapter 1 - How Growing Vegetables Can Save You Money ....

Chapter 2 - Vegetable Gardens - An Old Idea ....

Chapter 3 - Growing Vegetables From Seeds Or Plants ..

Chapter 4 - What to grow ....

Chapter 5 - Measuring the garden area ....

Chapter 6 - Preparing the soil ....

Chapter 7 - Proper planting ....

Chapter 8 - Caring for growing plants ....

Chapter 9 - How to harvest plants ....

Chapter 10 - Preserving vegetables and fruits ....

Chapter 11 - Creating a root cellar ....

Chapter 12 - Indoor gardens for herbs ....

Chapter 13 - How much can you save? ....

CHAPTER 1

HOW GROWING VEGETABLES
CAN SAVE YOU MONEY

If you are like most people, you are looking for a way to cut corners and save some money. There are a few things that you can do to save money today. You can travel less and use less gasoline. You can cut down on utility expenses by not using so much electricity and heat. You can eliminate eating out and eat at home. Perhaps you are already doing this but need to save more money. One way that you can save a lot of money is with your food bill. And with food prices going up, this may end up being a necessity. Not only can you save money on your food bill, but you can also start eating healthier.

You have probably heard about organic foods. These are foods that are all natural and do not contain any chemicals or preservatives. Organic vegetables are in your local supermarket and usually cost a lot more than the other vegetables that are grown using chemical pesticides and other toxins. You have probably heard that organic vegetables are better for you, but do not want to spend the extra money. After all, the idea is to save money - right? So spending extra money on organic vegetables, that are usually smaller than other vegetables can seem like a bad financial deal. And if you are like most of us, you are looking to get more bang out of your buck. Especially at the supermarket.

The way to really save money and eat healthy at the same time is to grow your own vegetables. This can trim your food bill substantially, depending on the amount of vegetables that you grow. If you have a patch of ground, you can save money by growing your own vegetables in the soil and wind up with vegetables and fruits that are healthier than those that you buy in the store. You can save at least $100 a month by growing your own vegetables and this savings, if you take the tips in this book, can be used after the harvest time if you learn how to preserve the various vegetables and fruits.

Think of what you can do with $100 a month. It can pay a couple of bills for you or just ease the burden for you a bit. And this savings can continue to blossom. You will see savings in your food bills every month when you start to grow your own vegetables. Of course, you will have to wait until harvest time to start to really start saving the money, but after your first harvest, you can save money all year long using the tips in this book. There are also tips that I will give you that will enable you to start saving money relatively soon with herbs.

It takes work to plant and harvest a vegetable garden, but it is good work. Working in a garden and planting vegetables or fruits is actually therapeutic. Many people enjoy being outdoors and gardening just for the heck of it. When you are saving money because of your endeavors, it makes the experience even better. The hard work is getting your garden started and harvesting as well as preserving the foods. Breaking this down, this consists of about 4 days out of the year. The rest is just maintenance. Four days is not much to ask when it comes to saving $100 a month on your grocery bills.

And best of all, you can start right now. Spring is the perfect planting time for a vegetable garden. By harvest time, which will be in July or August, you will be well on your way to start saving money.

If you are ready to start saving $100 a month in your food bill by growing your own vegetables, take the tips in this book and put them to use. Eat healthy foods and stop wasting your money at the grocery store.

CHAPTER 2

VEGETABLES GARDENS - AN OLD IDEA

Most of us today do not remember victory gardens. These were gardens that people planted during WWII to supplement rations during the war. During WWII, just about everything was rationed, including food. So people began to supplement that rationing with food from their own garden. Because the country was at war, the gardens that people used to supplement their war rations were dubbed Victory Gardens.

The country is currently at war with a recession. A war that requires a victory. Isn't it about time for Victory Gardens again? Just as our grandparents and great grandparents created victory gardens during WWII, we can do the same today. We aren't on food rations, although some of us might as well be. With an increasing number of people losing their jobs and facing home foreclosures, some of us may be rationing ourselves.

We don't have to feel helpless in the face of recession. We can do something about it. We can declare victory against the recession by planting our own victory gardens. All you need is a plot of soil and plants. The cost to prepare a garden is minimal, especially when you consider that it can save you $100 a month or more by growing your own vegetables.

A brief word about me:

I am too young for victory gardens, but I can remember my grandmother telling me about having a victory garden during the War. I never paid it much mind and never planted anything until a year ago, when I lost my job.

Like many others, my job was just downsized. I was able to get another job, but it paid a lot less money. And my kids and I were just managing to get by. I wanted to feed them healthy foods, but it seemed as though everything that was healthy was out of my price range. I didn't like the way we were eating and looked for various ways to save money.

I a way, I was like my grandmother. She was also a woman alone with two kids during WWII. Her husband was off fighting in the Pacific. She had to make do on rations and, being a city women for most of her life, knew nothing about gardening. But she managed to create a spectacular victory garden that was the envy of the neighbors. She not only was able to supplement her own rations, but those of her neighbors as well.

I saw myself as my grandmother - a single mom struggling to raise two kids and put food on the table.

Someone who didn't have much experience when it came to gardening. Okay - zero experience. But they say necessity is the mother of invention so I decided to re-invent myself. I created my own victory garden.

Not only was I able to save money as soon as those crops came in, but because I was using natural fertilizer to keep away bugs and rabbits, I felt as if I was feeding my kids healthier foods as well. I knew for a fact that my vegetables were organic because I was growing them myself. By September, I started to figure out the savings and they came up to $100 a month off of my grocery bills. This year, I plan to save even more.

The way that I figure it, if I can do it, anyone can do it. So many of my neighbors and friends asked me how I was able to manage so well, and make the transformation from being a city girl to being an expert gardener that I decided to write it down in a book.

By reading this book and following the step by step instructions that I have laid out for you, you too can create your very own victory garden.

Declare victory against the recession with your own victory garden!

CHAPTER 3

GROWING VEGETABLES FROM SEEDS OR PLANTS

If you are planning on starting a vegetable garden to save money the first thing that you need to consider is whether you are going to start from seeds or plants. Seeds are much less expensive, but take longer to grow. You need to grow plants from seeds in an indoor environment if you live in a four season climate. If you are planning on planting your garden soon for a late summer harvest, then you need to use plants. You can buy vegetable plants at any gardening center. They are much sturdier to put into the ground and have a better chance of taking root and producing vegetables. There are pros and cons to using both seeds and plants when it comes to growing your own vegetables.

Seeds - Pros and Cons

Seed come in packets and you can purchase them at most gardening and big box stores. The best aspects about using seeds is that you can grow them yourself into plants in your own home and make sure that the soil you use as well as any plant food used is organic. The seeds are also much less expensive than plants. There is also the satisfaction that you will gain when you are growing your own seeds for your plants.

The negative aspects about seeds is that you need more time to grow them so that they can take root. If you live in a four season climate, you need to grow the seeds indoors so that they can grow into sturdy plants before you can put them in the ground.

If you live in a climate that is warm, you can put down seeds and get them to grow into plants after sowing them in the ground. Seeds are also used for larger garden areas as it would be impractical to use plants.

Plants - Pros and Cons

You can find plants that can be used for your vegetable garden in any garden store. They are ready to plant and will produce fruit or vegetables. Plants are easy to use and if this is your first garden, they can be easier to space. Plant are already sturdy enough to be transferred to the ground and will bear fruit or vegetables.

The negative aspect of using plants is the cost. They tend to cost more than seeds. They are also often grown in soil that is filled with pesticides. If you decide to use plants instead of seeds, look for those that have been grown organically.

If you are a first time gardener, you may prefer to use plants over seeds. What many gardeners do, and what I did, is to use plants in your first garden so that you can get the garden seasoned and become familiar with planting and harvesting. Then the next year, you can cultivate your own plants from seeds.

Remember that if you live in a four season climate, you will want to use plants for your first garden as they have already taken root and are easier to grow. As you become more adept at gardening, you an start to easily grow vegetables from seeds.

CHAPTER 4

WHAT TO GROW

After you have figured out the concept of planting with seeds or plants, you can then decide what you want to grow. Naturally, for your first project you will want to make it easy on yourself. Some of the easiest fruits and vegetables that you can grow include the following:

- Tomatoes
- Peppers
- Cucumbers
- Onions
- Eggplant
- Potatoes
- Lettuce
- Squash (including pumpkins)
- Turnips

- Carrots
- Lima beans
- Corn
- Broccoli

These are all easy fruits and vegetables to grow. As we all have been told hundreds of times since childhood, tomatoes are a fruit and not a vegetable, so we will call them what they are, although for all intent purposes, they are treated and eaten as vegetables.

Tomatoes are the easiest of all of the fruits/vegetables to grow. Not only that, but they are also easy to can. We will talk about preserving vegetables for use throughout the year in later chapters. Suffice to say, that tomatoes, because they are fruits, are easy to can using a hot water bath.

You can find a garden store close to home or one that is online. If you live in a four season climate, chances are that you will be able to grow all of the above and more These are the vegetables that you want to get started with.

Of course, if you plan to grow all of these vegetables, you will need a sizeable garden. You can choose the vegetables that your family eats most of all of the time and grow them. You should also consider storage. Growing lettuce, for example, is great for salads and relatively easy to do, but it does not freeze or preserve. Turnips, carrots, onions and potatoes will keep well in a root cellar and will store for the winter. If you do not have a root cellar, you can make one when you follow the instructions that are in this book. It's not hard and just takes a bid of digging and keeping an area water proof. If you have your own cellar, you can save the trouble.

The worst thing that you can do when you are starting your own garden, is to get overwhelmed by planting too many vegetables. Think of those that you buy often, or would like to buy often, and go with them. As for me, I chose the root vegetables, tomatoes, peppers and broccoli. This year, I will grow squash and corn along with the vegetables I grew last year. I am also growing several vegetables from seeds.

Start out with a few vegetables that you eat often and each year, add a new vegetable to your garden. By growing the vegetables that you use often, you can save a lot of money every month on your food bill. The amount of money that you save each month will depend on how large the garden and how many vegetables you consume. Remember that you will be saving some of them, in various ways, to use for the winter months spring before the next harvest.

Space is a factor when you are planning your vegetable garden. Some vegetables or fruits, such as tomatoes and peppers, do not require a lot of room for growth. Root vegetables are also easy to grow as they grow down into the ground and do not take up a lot of room. Corn and squash take a lot more space so you may have to clear more room for them.

Another factor that you have to consider when you are growing vegetables to save money is that they may not look like those you see in the store. Many vegetables that are grown for mass production are aided with food dyes and waxed so that they look more attractive in the store. Your home grown vegetables are not likely to be as large, or as colorful, as the vegetables that you grow in the store. But they will be organic and healthier. And when it comes to taste, they will also taste just as good if not better than those that you purchase in the store.

Once you have established the vegetables that you are planning on growing, you must then learn the planting and harvesting times for these vegetables. Most vegetables are planted in the early to late spring, after the weather breaks and it is not likely to have a frost. Harvest time for most vegetables comes in early to late summer to early fall, depending on the vegetables. Tomatoes, for example, will be harvested early. As will peppers and cucumbers and some squash, as zucchini. Other vegetables are harvested a bit later such as the root vegetables.

Usually, the longer you can keep them in the ground, the better. When the leaves start to get brittle, it is time to dig them up. Corn and squash are autumn harvest, such as pumpkins and butternut squash. Lettuce and eggplants are harvested in late summer and early autumn.

Much depends on the region where you live. In some areas of the country, you can get corn in August. Tomatoes are usually harvested from July to August, but can be later in some parts of the country, especially in the warmer weather. There are different rules for harvesting on the East Coast than there are in the Midwest regions of the country. Here is a list of when you can (roughly) expect to harvest the above mentioned vegetables:

•Tomatoes - Harvest in early summer to late summer (July and August).

•Peppers - Harvest in mid summer to early autumn (Late July to September)

•Cucumbers - Harvest in mid summer to early autumn (Late July to September)

•Onions - Harvest in mid to late summer (August to early September)

•Eggplant - Harvest in mid summer to late summer (Late July to August)

•Potatoes - Harvest in early autumn to late autumn (September to early October)

•Lettuce - Harvest in Late summer (August to early September)

•Squash - Harvest in early to late autumn (late September to mid October)

•Turnips - Harvest in mid autumn (September)

•Carrots - Harvest in mid autumn (September)

•Lima Beans - Harvest in mid summer (August)

•Corn - Harvest in late August (in some areas) to September

•Broccoli - Harvest in mid to late summer (August to early September)

Once you have an idea of what you want to grow and when you can expect the vegetables (or fruits) to be ready for harvest, you can then start getting your garden ready to grow.

CHAPTER 5

MEASURING THE GARDEN AREA

The amount of garden area that you need depends on what you plan to grow in your garden as well as the amount of space that you have in which to create a garden. While some people make do with a small patch of land, you have most likely seen others who have an entire back yard devoted to gardening. My advice to you is this - use up as much space as you can spare. The tips given in this book will not only help you save money because you are growing fresh vegetables instead of buying them, but it will also save money when it comes to storing them.

A friend of mine decide one year to have a tomato garden. This was a long time ago, before I knew anything about gardening or how to preserve certain foods. She and her husband planted 40 tomato plants in their garden. The entire garden consisted of tomatoes.

If you have never grown anything, you should know that tomatoes are the easiest of all of the garden vegetables (even though it's a fruit) to grow. Her tomatoes came out in full bloom and then started producing fruit. Pretty soon, my friend was giving tomatoes to just about everyone she knew, including the mailman. The entire neighborhood was tomatoes out and she vowed not to do this again. A great many tomatoes went to waste and a great deal of bunnies were happy. But this didn't have to be the case.

Had my friend known that canning tomatoes is one of the simplest of all garden fruit and vegetables preservation, she could have had tomatoes, sauce, salsa and just about anything for the entire year.

IF YOU HAVE THE GROUND - PLANT THE VEGETABLES

If you have the ground, plant the vegetables. Always consider that some plants may not do well. Despite your best efforts, some crops will be eaten by sneaky critters like rabbits (although I will give you tips on how to deal with that) and some will just not work out. Every garden has duds.

While you do not want to start out with a garden that is overwhelming and takes up your entire backyard, you do not want to have a small garden that only produces a few fruits and vegetables and does not really save you any money. Remember, your victory garden should be one that will save you money not only in the months of the harvest, but for the year afterward. So you need to have plenty of room.

Section off a piece of land in your yard where the garden will grow. Bear in mind that certain vegetables, like corn and potatoes, take more room in which to grow. Tomatoes grow up and can be confined to a smaller space. Others, especially the root vegetables, need a foot between them to grow properly and not get entangled in the ground.

Also keep in mind that you need to have space between the rows of crops in order to maintain the garden. A friend of mine had a great idea to build a tomato garden in a small patch of ground on the side of the house. She figured she could get 10 tomato plants in their easily. She planted them, watered them, made sure they climbed their cages, but had no where to walk. Once the tomatoes had grown, she couldn't get into the garden without stepping all over the plants. Do not let this happen to you. You need to have rows between the crops where you can work so that you can properly maintain the growing crops and, when harvest time comes, harvest them as well.

After you have marked off the area where you are going to plan your garden, you need to then start to prepare the supplies you will need to get the garden going. You can get the following supplies from the garden store, or borrow them from a neighbor:

•Garden gloves. You will need these throughout your gardening, so be sure to get a good pair.

•Garden Hoe

•Garden Spade

•Wheelbarrow

•Garden rake

•Chicken wire or some fencing material to keep the garden contained and the animals out.

These are the materials that you will need to dig up the garden and get it ready for planting. Some people rent a rototiller to turn over the soil in the garden. This does the job quickly in a large vegetable garden, but costs money to rent. It is also a heavy piece of machinery and can be difficult to maneuver. I always preferred using the old fashioned garden tools, but if you are strong enough to use this battery operated or electrical power device, then you might want to go for it. You are going to need to turn the soil over in order to get it prepared for gardening.

Also, take a look at the dirt that you have under your lawn. Chances are it is black dirt, like clay. This is difficult soil in which to grow crops. You need to have good soil and may want to pick up some bags of potting soil for your crops. If the dirt is hard and seems like clay, then you need to mix in some good top so that your vegetables will grow. As you continue to grow the garden, the more nutrient rich the soil will become. As years go on, the garden soil takes on a life of its own so that you will not need top soil.

It is a good idea to stake off where you want to have your garden with some stakes and string. This way you know where you plan to dig and will have an even looking garden. After you have prepared the area by sectioning it off and getting the necessary supplies that you need to prepare the garden, you can then start digging.

CHAPTER 6

PREPARING THE SOIL

This is the hardest part of growing your own vegetables. It is hard labor to dig up the soil and turn it. It is even more difficult if you have grass or rocks in the place where you want to have your garden. If you have grass, for example, you will want to dig up the grass and put it in the wheelbarrow, taking it to a compost heap in your yard and getting rid of it. You are going to need a lot more soil in the area as you will have several inches dug into the ground when you are finished.

Use the wheelbarrow to transport the grass or weeds that you did up and get rid of them. The soil for your garden should be as pure as possible and devoid of any weeds, rocks or clay. If you are stuck with clay under the grass, you can turn it over with the spade and mix in some good top soil.

START BY DIGGING

Start by digging out a small section of the ground and continue going until you have dug up the entire garden. It is best to do this a day after a rain. Not just after a rain, otherwise it will be very muddy. But if you do this after it has rained within a few days, the ground will be a lot softer and easier to manage.

Once you get rid of all of the rocks, weeds and grass, you can then start to turn over the soil. You do this by using the spade to dig up the soil and then flipping it over. You should do this throughout the entire garden. You can use the end of the spade to chop up any clumps in the soil. The soil needs to be as smooth as possible before you plant.

After you have turned over all of the soil, use the garden hoe to chop up the soil even more. You can make the soil have a fine consistency if you so choose, but you have to work at it. You have to keep chopping and tilling the soil.

If you want to have the best results with your vegetable garden, you need to get the soil to the point where it falls easily between your hands when you pick it up. The two ways to do this is to dig out the garden a half a foot down and fill it with top soil, or use the soil that you have, chopping it up as much as you can before you plant. The latter is the least expensive option and, despite the fact that it sounds difficult, is just as hard as digging into the ground and pulling up clay.

USE TOP SOIL

Once you have the soil to the point where it has all been turned over and chopped up, is rid of clumps of dirt, rocks and weeds or grass, you can then add several bags of top soil to the mix. Top soil is a fine grain of soil that will enable your plants grow even better. You can also choose fertilizer soil. This will also allow your plants to grow well. You want to give your plants a boost by adding in a store bought soil as this will make it easier for them to adjust to their new home. Fertilizer may not seem like something that you want to handle, but it is organic and does work very well to allow for plants to grow to their maximum potential.

After you have added bags of top soil or fertilizer, take the garden rake and then smooth the ground over. You should use the rake to mix in all of the soil and make sure that the soil is flat and easy for planting. It should be loose but even.

CREATE ROWS FOR WALKING

Once you have done this, you can make rows between the areas where you want to plant the crops. The crops should sit up higher than these rows that will allow you to walk between the crops for maintenance, and also allow any rain to fall off into the rows. Creating mini-drainage ditches in your garden is not absolutely necessary, but can help you if you live in an area where there is a lot of rain. While water is naturally important for crops to grow, too much can end up flooding out your garden. In most areas, there is not a lot of rain in the summer months, so this is not crucial. Be sure, however, to visualize a row between the planting rows where you will be able to walk and take care of the plants as well as harvest the vegetables that grow in the garden.

PROTECT YOUR GARDEN FROM ANIMALS

Once you have properly tilled the soil and prepared it for planting, you need to use chicken wire or some sort of fencing around the garden area. This will keep the rabbits and other critters out of your garden. Rabbits will have a field day with your crops if you do not protect them. If you are growing vegetables to save money, it hardly makes sense to give away half of your crops to the rabbits.

Chicken wire will keep out any animals such as rabbits, raccoons or possum in the area. It may not look attractive, but you can always back it up with a more attractive looking picket fence if you feel the need. Just remember that the wooden fences are useless when it comes to keeping out rabbits and other creatures as they gnaw right through. Chicken wire will protect your garden from animals.

After you have quartered off the garden with your wire and the soil is ready for planting, you are ready to start planting your vegetables.

CHAPTER 7

PROPER PLANTING

Proper planting for your garden is needed for your vegetables to take root and thrive. You must space them apart the proper distance in the soil and also take any other precautions that are needed to get them to grow. You should have a foot between each of the plants that you are planting in your garden, and a foot and half between corn and pumpkins. It may look silly at first, when you plant your garden, to see the plants so far apart. But as the plants grow from tiny plants to large plants, you will start to see the difference.

Before you start planting your vegetables in your vegetable garden, make sure that you have the following:

•Garden gloves

•Hand spade

•Potting soil

•Wheelbarrow

If you are borrowing a wheelbarrow from a neighbor, you are going to want to borrow it again for planting. You can transport all of your plants at once to the garden area and then plant them. A wheelbarrow is not a very expensive investment for a gardener and can help you even when it comes time for harvest. Assuming that you have a place to keep the wheelbarrow, you will have many uses for this product.

If at all possible, you should schedule your planting for before a rain. You want to make sure that the weather is on an even keel and that there should not be any more frosts. Ideally, the ground should be dewy when you get up in the morning so that the crops will get plenty of moisture. As the weather gets warmer, you will most likely not have this dew in the morning and you will have to pay close attention to hydrating the crops.

When you are planting from plants, you will need to dig a hole in the ground with a hand spade that is deep enough for the plant. You want to leave as much of the original soil around the plant in which it grew so it can get used to the new earth. Planting takes time and patience and you want to be sure that you are spacing the plants properly. Use potting soil around the plant to make it even more fine and inviting for the plant.

Depending on the size of the garden, planting the garden can take you a day, or at least the better part of the sunlight. For the most part, the preparation and planting of the garden can be done in one nice weekend. Once you have planted the plants into the ground, you will then want to water them and also feed them.

FEEDING THE PLANTS

You can buy plant feeder for vegetables at your local gardening store. You put it in a container and then squirt it onto the plants. Look for all natural, organic products that will help your plants grow even stronger. For the most part, however, the vegetables will grow as long as they get sunlight and water. These are the two main components to healthy plants. And each year, the soil will become even more enriched with vitamins and minerals and easier for plants to grow.

You can also use spikes in the ground that can add as plant feeders. Spikes can be a bit more costly, but they can add the necessary nutrients to the soil that your plants need to get the most growth. You can add spikes to the plants once a week to keep them growing strong.

Some plants, such as tomato plants, need to have sticks or cages around them so that they can grow up. While most vegetables grow close to the ground, tomatoes are a fruit that grows on a vine. You need to put special cages or sticks to get the tomato plants off of the ground and growing up. This will enable the plants to blossom and them form the fruit.

TOMATO CAGES

Get some cheap tomato cages at the gardening store. These are made of wire and will last for years. Place each of these cages around each tomato plant. As the tomato plants continue to grow, you can use twist ties to fasten the plant to the cages, forcing it to grow upright instead of laying on the ground. While you can use sticks for the same purpose, cages are easy to use, easy to put into the ground and work better. Sticks only offer one way up, but cages allow the plant to flourish. Put the tomato cages in the ground, surrounding the plant, after you plant them. It will then be easier to start to get the vine to creep up the cages as the plant continues to grow.

Once you have completed your planting, water your garden. You want to water it so that the water puddles a bit in the garden, but not so that it is drenched. You should also look for the weather report to see if you expect rain. If rain is expected, water the garden a little bit and then let Mother Nature take its course and water the garden for you. Once the garden has been planted, you need to make sure that it remains hydrated, fed and secure from animals.

CHAPTER 8

CARING FOR GROWING PLANTS

Caring for growing plants require that you look after them on a daily basis. Not only do you have to make sure that they are watered, but you also have to remove any weeds that grow in the garden that will choke the nutrients from your plants. In order to care for growing plants, you need the following equipment:

- Plant feeder
- Watering can or hose with gentle spray
- Hand hoe
- Gardening gloves

Each day, you will want to take a look at your garden to see how your plants are doing. You should pull any weeds that are in the ground as well as water the garden. While you will not need to water the garden after rain, obviously, you will still want to look at the garden after a rainfall to see if the plants are stable and to pull any weeds. Remember that weeds will grow just as much if not more in the setting you have created.

If you look at your garden every day and tend to it, you will have less of a problem with maintenance. Your routine should be to take a look at the garden each night, just as the sun goes down and it is settling into dusk. It is best to water the garden at this time, rather than in the hot sun as the plants can burn. The plants should always be hydrated, but not soaking. While there is nothing that you can do about rainstorms, you do not want to always be soaking your plants.

Feed the plants regularly with plant food that is organic. You can get a plant food spreader that looks like a plastic bottle with a hose attached to it to spray your plants. This will give them additional nutrients and provide you with better vegetables. Feed the plants once a week for best results.

GET RID OF INSECTS!

Insects can play havoc around your plants and rabbits are very ornery creatures that tend to go through great extremes to get at those vegetables. One way that you can scare off rabbits is to trick the creatures into thinking that their natural predators are around. Rabbits are afraid of cats and dogs, two animals that prey on them. You can buy a spray that smells like the scent of dog or cat urine and put it around the area surrounding the garden. This should keep rabbits and other animals at bay.

Insects can be more problematic and many people resort to using pesticides to get rid of insects that will eat the leaves and can harm the plants. Pesticides are usually a bad idea. While commercial farmers dust crops using pesticides, they contain benzene, a carcinogen, and are not something that you want to have around. You are better off to use either a natural spray to get rid of bugs such as a citronella. Some bugs, like the hornworm, a bug that attacks tomato bushes, are hard to get rid of even with pesticides. Natural sprays will help get rid of some bugs and keep others from doing too much damage. While you naturally want to grow as many crops as you can and save as much money as you can when it comes to buying vegetables for your grocery bill, you do not want to do it at the expense of your own health or that of your family. Accept the fact that some crops will get attacked, but not many if you are out there diligently using all natural products to rid the plants of bugs and remove weeds.

GET RID OF WEEDS!

Remember to pull weeds as soon as you see them. If it is too difficult for you to pull weeds every night when you get home from work, you should make it a habit to pull them once a week. Again, it is better to pull weeds after the rain as they will come up easily. The weeds must be pulled by the roots in order for it to make any difference. Use garden gloves and a garden hoe to pull up weeds and get rid of them. Put all weeds into a compost pile.

If you see earthworms while you are tending to your garden, do not kill them. They are actually a gardener's best friend, despite the fact that they are slimy and not much to look at. They do not harm the crops. In fact, they turn the soil so that the crops aerate even better. Earthworms are often found in bags of top soil.

MAKE SURE SOIL DOES NOT ERODE

Speaking of soil, check the soil around the plants to see if some of it has eroded. In some cases, rains will erode some of the soil around your plants, making it difficult for them to grow. You should always have a bag of top soil or potting soil on hand to put around the plants, especially after the rain, so that they can continue to grow.

If you tend to your garden on a regular basis, you can expect good results. One of the problems that most people have with gardens is that they plant them and then forget about them.

Or they see bugs and think that the entire garden is infested. Or they don't want to pull weeds. Despite neglect, some vegetables will still grow, but you will not get the results that you need and certainly not be able to save substantial amounts of money on your food bill if you do not maintain your garden regularly. You will find that this not only allows you to save money for your family on the grocery bill, but it will also give you a sense of peace.

FIND PEACE IN THE GARDEN

One of the things that the bad economy has brought out in people is anxiety and stress over money. An increasing number of people are going to the doctor for anxiety and stress and are worried over money. Most people who find themselves sitting in the waiting room of the doctor's office will end up walking out of that office with some sort of prescription. Instead of taking drugs because you are worried about the economy, you can actually do something about it and start gardening.

Gardening is more than just a useful hobby that can help you save money on your food bill by growing vegetables. It is actually a way to relieve stress and find peace. Most people who garden report that they lose themselves in the gardening process and find peace. This is not only a way to grow vegetables, but also a way to get outside, do something physical and get relief from stress. You cannot lose when it comes to gardening in your own vegetable garden.

Take care of your garden regularly and it will take care of you. By looking after it, watering it, making sure that the weeds are pulled and that it remains insect and bunny free, you can look forward to a nice harvest.

CHAPTER 9

HOW TO HARVEST PLANTS

All of your hard work has paid off and you actually have a bunch of vegetables grown in your garden. You can look to the chart written earlier as to when you can expect them to come in, although you will know when they are ready simply by looking at them. Root vegetables are a bit more difficult to tell when they are ready, although you can usually tell by the maturity of the leaves and vines on the ground. Onions, for example, will have very firm stalks.

Tomatoes will continue to keep coming. They are different than other vegetables in that they tend to produce more rapidly. You can start removing tomatoes from the vines as soon as you see them grow a bit red. One way that you can allow them to get red is to pick them when they are slightly orange and then leave them in the sun. They will grow a nice shade of red.

Start looking towards your early to mid summer harvest vegetables right away and taking them out of the garden and into your home. If you are like most people, you will have an abundance of tomatoes. The early summer vegetables need to be preserved quickly as they will not sit around for months on end. You should use bushel baskets to collect your vegetable harvest and plan how you want to preserve them.

Harvest time entails a lot more work than planting time. While preparing a garden and planting can easily be accomplished in a weekend, a proper harvest takes more than just pulling vegetables off of the vines and out of the ground and cooking them. It means preserving them for the winter. Remember, the purpose of your "victory garden" is to gain a victory over the bad economy and save $100 a month on your food bill. You may even save more if you plant more.

As soon as the vegetables start coming in, start to use them in meals. In order to save as much money on your food bill as possible, you should incorporate as many vegetables as you can in every meal. You can prepare them in a number of different ways in order to provide your family with treats that are good for them, totally organic and filling. In the next chapter we will deal with how you can preserve these vegetables for later use. For now, we will talk about the harvest.

WHAT IS A HARVEST LIKE?

The harvest of the vegetables is not like you see on TV. The crops come in at different times and you will most likely always be pulling something from the garden. You will have a ball coming up with exciting summer recipes that incorporate the use of these crops. But despite the fact that you and your family are eating more vegetables and you are saving on your food bill, you are still going to have some left over.

Keep the harvested vegetables in a cool, dry place until you are ready to preserve them for future use. Many people choose to use weekend time to "put up" vegetables so that they can be used throughout the year. Until you are ready to deal with the vegetables, you should be sure to harvest them as they grow so that you can continue to reap the harvest and more vegetables will grow in their place. When you are cooking vegetables to eat, be sure to use the first picked so that you keep the freshest vegetables for canning, freezing or pickling.

Tomatoes are the fastest growing and are the most versatile when it comes to meals. You can make spaghetti sauce, salsa or salads - just to name a few things - with tomatoes. As time wears on and you continue to garden, you can even learn to make your own ketchup and tomato paste using the tomatoes from your garden.

Green tomatoes can be a tasty treat if you fry them. Wash a green tomato and cut it in round slices. Dip each slice into a beaten egg and then coat it with bread crumbs mixed with shredded Parmesan cheese. Fry in olive oil until brown on each side. This is a tasty treat and filling.

You can also do the same thing with eggplant that you grow from your garden, although you will want to peal the eggplant first. Eggplant can be used as a meat as it is so thick and filling. You can make an eggplant veggie burger for a meal.

Use the vegetables that you harvest from your garden and store those that are not in use in a cool dry place. On weekends, you can start to can or preserve vegetables so that they are ready for the upcoming months. Two of the earliest vegetables that you will be canning or preserving will be tomatoes and cucumbers. Others early vegetables that will need to be preserved early, while you are still harvesting the later summer vegetables are peppers and onions. You will most likely be working to preserve each weekend in the months of August and September. This is all part of the harvest and will allow you to make the most of your vegetable garden and save money on future food bills. Once you get used to doing this, you will be able to save even more money as you will most likely branch out and grow more vegetables and fruits.

The harvest time is a time for much work, but it is all worth it. Preserving vegetables and fruits may seem daunting at first, but is really easy once you get the hang of it. You can also just freeze vegetables as well, making it very simple to preserve them.

One of the reasons why people had parties after a harvest was to celebrate the crops they harvested that year as well as treat themselves for a job well done. Once your harvest is over, you will have plenty of vegetables to last you until next year and you and your family can not only save money each month on your food bill, but will also be eating healthier.

CHAPTER 10

PRESERVING VEGETABLES AND FRUITS

There are many ways that you can preserve vegetables and fruits. Fruits are often cooked and then canned, such as jellies, jams and preserves. Fruits are easy to can and only need to undergo a hot water process that seals the wax on the ring of the canning jar. This is easy to do. Tomatoes can be canned in this manner.

Preserving vegetables, however, is another matter. Canning vegetables requires a pressure cooker and a lot of knowledge. You can get Botulism from not canning vegetables properly. Unless you have experience with using a pressure cooker, you are better off to preserve vegetables in different ways such as pickling or freezing. Each vegetable and fruit has different ways that are ideal for preservation. Here is a run down on all of the different ways that you can preserve vegetables that you have grown in your garden and save money:

Canning

This process works best with tomatoes. You need to use sterilized canning jars with wax rings and lids. Wash the jars in the dishwasher before adding the tomatoes. The tomatoes should be washed and peeled. To peel a tomato, put it in hot water and it will easily peel in your hands. You should put the tomatoes in the jars and fill up with sterile water. Put on the rings and lids and boil the jars in a canning pot for 20 minutes. After you remove them from the canning pot, you should hear the lids making a slight pop noise that means they are sealed.

You can also cook the tomatoes and add spices to make salsa or spaghetti sauces, or just cooked tomatoes, and also use the same process. The main concern is to make sure all instruments and jars are sterile. You can buy canning jars and pots at your grocery store. Once sealed, the jars should be stored in a cool, dark place and can be used throughout the year.

Pickling

Pickling is used for cucumbers and onions and involves using sea salts and vinegar to preserve the vegetables for a period of time. Pickling can also be accomplished using alcohol, although this is rarely done with vegetables. In order to pickle any vegetables, you need to follow the same process as in canning with regard to sterilization, and then do the hot water bath. Because they are preserved in alcohol, you do not have to worry about bacteria forming. Use the hot water bath to make sure the jars are sealed and then sore in a cool, dry place.

Freezing

Freezing is one of the easiest ways that you can preserve vegetables. Many people who want to save money on their grocery bills invest in a deep freezer. This can store all of the vegetables for you. You need to use containers or freezer bags that will lock out air and preserve the vegetables. Place cleaned vegetables in the freezer bags or containers and stick them in the freezer after sealing. This only takes a few minute and works well with corn, peppers, eggplant, broccoli and carrots. It does not work for lettuce or potatoes. Lettuce will turn to mush in the freezer and potatoes will get black.

Root Cellar

Root vegetables such as onions, potatoes, turnips and carrots can be stored in a root cellar for the entire year. If you do not have a root cellar, read the next chapter and you can learn how you can create your own root cellar to store your vegetables. You can also store them in a basement, provided it is cool and unheated. Root vegetables can last a year if properly stores, but it has to be in a cool and dark place.

By preserving as many as the vegetables as you can, you will be able to continue to save money throughout the year with the vegetables that you have grown in your own garden.

CHAPTER 11

CREATING A ROOT CELLAR

A root cellar was used to store vegetables as well as other food supplies long before electricity came along. Today, because so many people are looking for a way to save money and eat healthier, organic foods by growing their own vegetables, many people are creating their own root cellars. This requires a parcel of ground where you can dig down and line with rocks. Many people create roots cellars in their back yards under a shed. You would have a latch door in the floor of the shed that opens and allows you to step down a small ladder into the root cellar.

The root cellar has to be covered to avoid any type of accidents or any animal getting into the cellar. You should line the walls and floor of the root cellar with stones to prevent bugs from getting into the cellar. Products that are stored in the root cellar should be stored in brown sacks to further protect them from rain or insects. The root cellar should be covered at all times when not in use.

Before you start digging on your property, call out your local utility companies so that they can mark out where your utilities are located. You never want to dig on your property unless you know where the utilities are located so that you do not uproot a wire or cable.

A root cellar will enable you to store turnips, carrots, potatoes, onions and squash for longer periods of time. If you live in a house where you have a cellar, you can usually use this as your root cellar. You can even create your own root cellar indoors by using a wood container that you make yourself to store the vegetables. This container can be kept in a cool, dark place (preferably the basement) to store your vegetables. There are "build your own root cellar" kits online that you can use for this purpose. You will probably find this easier than digging your own root cellar on your property.

If you do not have room for a root cellar, you can cook potatoes and freeze them instead of storing them in a root cellar. Turnips and carrots can be frozen uncooked and will be fine. Be sure to peel them before freezing.

A root cellar is the ideal place to store all of your preserved foods as it is cool and dark. Whether you decide to quarter off part of the basement to build a root cellar for your vegetables or build your on, you will find that all of your root vegetables have much more staying power when you store them in a cool, dark place.

CHAPTER 12

INDOOR GARDENS FOR HERBS

While you're saving a ton of money by growing your own vegetables, you can even save more money by growing your own herbs. The beauty about growing herbs is that you can grow them indoors and all year long. Most herbs just need a little bit of sunlight and water and will grow just fine.

Herbs will flavor your foods in a totally natural way and can also be dried or frozen for later use. Fresh herbs, when mixed with the vegetables from your garden, can make for delicious and healthy meals for your family. Not only will you save money at the grocery store, but you will find that fresh herbs taste better than the freeze dried variety that you find in the store. And they are completely natural, organic and have no preservatives.

You can grow herbs from seeds in your own indoor herb garden. You just need to find a place where you will keep your garden and where it will be safe from spilling due to children and pets. You can purchase a kit to grow herbs or just grow them yourself. You just need potting containers, soil and seeds. Plant the seeds deep into the soil, or as directed on the seed packet, and water. Put the container in an area where it can get the most sunlight and water every day. As the herbs begin to mature, you can harvest the leaves from these plants and use them in different foods. They contain no pesticides and are completely natural. You do not have to preserve them as they can grow all year long. If you would like, you can always put them in a freezer bag and stick them in the freezer. Fresh herbs taste best and cost only pennies to grow.

GROW VEGETABLES FROM SEEDS

In addition to growing your fresh herbs indoors, you can also grow vegetables from seeds using the same concept. Growing vegetables from seeds can be done in the winter months so that the plants are ready to be transplanted into the garden in the spring. Every vegetable has a different growth time period, so follow the directions on the package of seeds as to when you plant. If you set aside an area in your home that gets an adequate amount of sunlight and is safe from children and pets, you can have an indoor garden for growing vegetable plants from seeds to save you even more money. Furthermore, because you grew them yourself, you know that they are free from any pesticides or toxins.

Growing vegetables from seeds is not difficult. Just make sure that you follow directions as to how much sunlight they need as well as the amount of water that they require. If you take care of the plants every day, chances are that you will have quite a few healthy, sturdy plants for your garden when it comes planting time.

GROW HERBS OUTDOORS, TOO!

While we talked earlier in this chapter about growing herbs indoors, they are not only for the indoors. You can grow herbs outdoors in the warm months as well. Many people enjoy growing herbs out of doors because they will grow larger and yield more benefits. It is always a good idea to plant a few herbs in your garden that you can harvest when you harvest the rest of the vegetables. If you are the type of person who dislikes growing any type of plant indoors, has small children and pets or just does not have adequate sunlight in your home, you can grow herbs outdoors and harvest them in the same way you would vegetables. Fresh herbs can be dried or frozen for preservation and use later on.

CHAPTER 13

HOW MUCH CAN YOU SAVE?

Once you get into vegetable gardening, you will find that you are not only having a good time, but saving money. Last year, I ended up saving $100 a month off of my food bill, but this year I plan to save even more.

After discussing my savings and techniques with friends who also like to garden, I found that they are saving even more money. One thing that all gardeners have told me is that the soil continues to get richer with each passing year, yielding better crops. You also get to know what your family will eat and won't eat when you are vegetable gardening and can skip some vegetables that are not very popular with the family.

Another thing that you learn as you go on with vegetable gardening is how much each crop yields. This is something that you have to see for yourself. I was unprepared as to how many tomatoes and cucumbers I was going to get last year, but this year, I know to plant less plants and more broccoli, as those plants did not yield as many vegetables. This will enable me to save even more money.

By growing my vegetable plants from seeds, I will also save more money. I discussed my techniques with those who have been growing their own vegetables for years and they laughed when I told them of my idea for a book - as they have known these secrets to gardening their entire lives and have always saved money. It amazes many who were brought up in the country to know that there are people out there like you and me who do not know that you can save money by growing your own vegetables.

The tips that you read in this book have been practiced not only by me, but by my mentors. They are easy enough for anyone to follow, but they do take work. The work will pay off for you when you see how healthy your family is eating as well as how much money you are saving.

While I saved $100 a month growing my own vegetables, I spoke to a friend who said she saves about $300 a month growing her own vegetables. Her family tends to eat a lot of vegetables because she has been growing them for a few years and they prefer to eat home grown products.

DECLARE VICTORY WITH YOUR OWN VICTORY GARDEN!

If you are fed up with the ever rising cost of food and the constant worry about the economy and job security, it is time that you do something about it. Instead of worrying, take action and declare victory against the recession with your own victory garden. Just like your grandparents or great grandparents did during WWII, you can supplement your food budget by growing your own vegetables at home and save at least $100 a month off of your food bill!

Printed by Libri Plureos GmbH in Hamburg, Germany